D1456865

LIFE STORIES

ABRAHAM LINCOLN

Gillian Gosman

PowerKiDS press™

New York

Published in 2011 by The Rosen Publishing Group, Inc.
29 East 21st Street, New York, NY 10010

First Edition

Editor: Jennifer Way   Spanish translation: Eduardo Alamán
Book Design: Ashley Burrell and Erica Clendening

Photo Credits: Cover (background, inset), pp. 4–5, 12, 14–15 FPG/Getty Images; pp. 6, 10, 16 SuperStock/Getty Images; pp. 6–7 Willis D. Vaughn/National Geographic/Getty Images; p. 20 Kean Collection/Getty Images; pp. 8–9, 18–19 Hulton Archive/Getty Images; pp. 10–11 Alan Copson/Getty Images; pp. 12–13 © www.iStockphoto.com/Steven Wynn; pp. 14, 22 (top) MPI/Getty Images; pp. 16–17 Time Life Pictures/Mansell/Getty Images; pp. 18, 22 (bottom) Stock Montage/Getty Images; pp. 20–21© www.iStockphoto.com/Gene Chutka.

Library of Congress Cataloging-in-Publication Data

Gosman, Gillian.
  Abraham Lincoln / by Gillian Gosman. — 1st ed.
    p. cm. — (Life stories)
  Includes index.
  ISBN 978-1-4488-2582-0 (library binding) — ISBN 978-1-4488-2753-4 (pbk.) —
ISBN 978-1-4488-2754-1 (6-pack)
  1. Lincoln, Abraham, 1809-1865—Juvenile literature. 2. Presidents—United States—Biography—Juvenile literature. I. Title.
  E457.905.G67 2011
  973.7092—dc22
  [B]
                                    2010034282

Manufactured in the United States of America
CPSIA Compliance Information: Batch #WW11PK: For Further Information contact Rosen Publishing, New York, New York at 1-800-237-9932

CONTENTS

Meet Abraham Lincoln

We know Abraham Lincoln as Honest Abe and the Illinois Rail-Splitter. These nicknames describe his simple childhood and his lifetime of hard work.

Abraham Lincoln grew up poor. He studied and worked hard and later became the United States' sixteenth president.

Lincoln stood his ground against the spread of **slavery**. He led the nation through a long and terrible war. He was a strong leader, a great speaker, and a thoughtful man. Many people believe he was the United States' greatest president.

Young Lincoln

Abraham Lincoln was born in Kentucky in a one-room cabin on February 12, 1809. His parents were poor **frontier** settlers. The family moved to Indiana when Abraham was seven. His mother died two years later.

Lincoln was a tall man. At 6 feet 4 inches (1.9 m) he stood taller than most men of his time.

This is the cabin in Kentucky where Lincoln lived as a child.

Sometimes, young Abraham went to school. Because his family was poor, Abraham sometimes had to work instead. He read in his free time. In 1830, the Lincoln family moved to Illinois.

Life in the Age of Expansion

Abraham Lincoln lived during a time when the United States was growing quickly. With this growth came disagreement. Southern farmers wanted to own slaves to work their fields. Many northerners believed slavery was wrong, though.

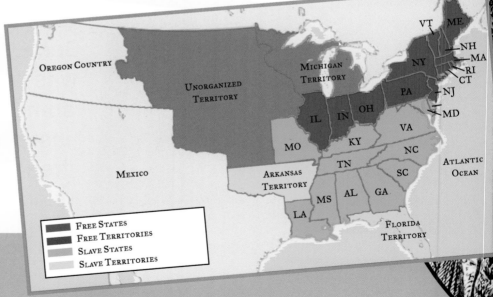

This map shows where slavery was allowed after the Missouri Compromise of 1820.

Slaves in the South worked on large farms called plantations.

The government made **compromises** to keep an even number of slave states and free states. The Missouri Compromise of 1820 allowed slavery in the new state of Missouri and outlawed slavery in the new state of Maine.

The Country Lawyer

In 1834, Lincoln was **elected** to the Illinois General Assembly. This is part of Illinois's state government. Lincoln also began to study law. In 1837, he opened his law office in Springfield.

Here is a painting of the Lincoln family from the 1860s. From left to right are Mary Todd, William, Robert, Thomas, and Abraham.

This is the house in which Lincoln and his family lived in Springfield.

Lincoln worked hard. His law partner said of Lincoln, "His **ambition** was a little engine that knew no rest." In 1842, Lincoln married Mary Todd. They had four sons. Only one, Robert, lived to be an adult, though.

Leader on the Rise

In 1858, Lincoln ran for **Congress** against Stephen A. Douglas. During the race, the two men held **debates**. Debates are public arguments about ideas. Lincoln and Douglas argued about slavery. Lincoln was against slavery. Douglas was for it.

There were a total of seven debates between Lincoln and Douglas. The debates became known as the Lincoln-Douglas debates.

Lincoln believed slavery was wrong. He also believed that keeping the United States together was his most important job as president.

Lincoln lost the election. The debates made him widely known, though. In 1860, he was chosen as the Republican **candidate** for president of the United States. He won the election.

A Country at War

After Lincoln was elected president, 11 states **seceded** and formed the Confederate States of America. The Confederate states were South Carolina, Mississippi, Florida, Alabama, Georgia, Louisiana, Texas, Virginia, Arkansas, Tennessee, and North Carolina.

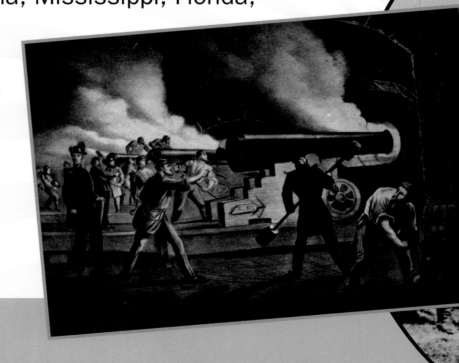

This picture shows Union, or Northern, troops fighting at Fort Sumter.

In this photograph, Lincoln (center) is meeting with Union troops.

On April 12, 1861, Confederate troops opened fire on Fort Sumter. The attack marked the beginning of the Civil War.

THE WARTIME PRESIDENT

The Civil War was long and bloody. The Union army of the North lost many battles. Lincoln had to make many hard decisions. On January 1, 1863, Lincoln freed the slaves of the Confederacy with the Emancipation Proclamation.

This painting shows Lincoln (third from left) reading the Emancipation Proclamation.

Lincoln gave the Gettysburg Address in 1863. He said the war was a fight for the country and for freedom.

In March 1863, Lincoln created a military draft. This law required that all healthy adult men serve in the armed forces. The draft made people angry and there were riots, or fighting, in New York City.

A Second Election

Lincoln was reelected in 1864. At his **inauguration** in 1865, Lincoln gave a powerful speech. He said that the Confederate states should not be punished when they rejoined the United States. He said that the

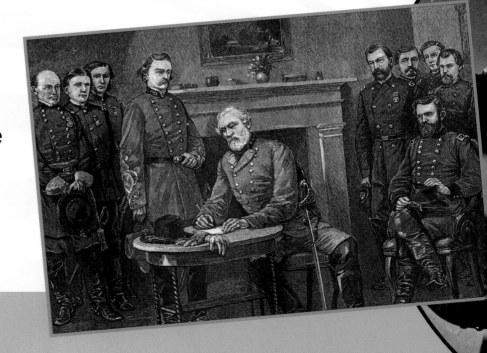

This picture shows Robert E. Lee (center) surrendering to Ulysses S. Grant (seated at right).

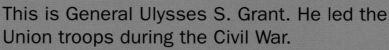
This is General Ulysses S. Grant. He led the Union troops during the Civil War.

nation would be stronger when it was once again united, or working together. On April 9, 1865, Confederate general Robert E. Lee **surrendered** to Union general Ulysses S. Grant. This brought the fighting of the war to an end.

Death at the Theater

On April 14, 1865, Lincoln was watching a play at Ford's Theater in Washington, D.C. During the play John Wilkes Booth shot Lincoln. Lincoln died early the next day.

This picture shows John Wilkes Booth (far left) coming up behind Lincoln (second from left).

This is the statue of Lincoln in the Lincoln Memorial in Washington, D.C.

Lincoln is remembered today as the president who saw the nation through the Civil War. He is also honored for helping bring an end to slavery in the United States.

TIMELINE

February 12, 1809

Lincoln is born in Kentucky.

1860

Lincoln is elected president of the United States.

April 12, 1861

Confederate troops open fire on Union forces at Fort Sumter.

April 14, 1865

Lincoln is shot by John Wilkes Booth. He dies the next day.

April 9, 1865

The Confederate forces surrender to the Union forces.

January 1, 1863

The Emancipation Proclamation frees all slaves in the Confederate states and territories.

Glossary

ambition (am-BIH-shun) The wish to do well.

candidate (KAN-dih-dayt) A person who runs in an election.

compromises (KOM-pruh-myz-ez) Things given up to reach an agreement.

Congress (KON-gres) The part of the U.S. government that makes laws.

debates (dih-BAYTS) Meetings at which different people or groups argue different points of view.

elected (ee-LEK-tid) Picked for an office by voters.

frontier (frun-TEER) The edge of a settled country, where the wilderness begins.

inauguration (ih-naw-gyuh-RAY-shun) The event of swearing in a government official.

seceded (sih-SEED-ed) Withdrew from a group or a country.

slavery (SLAY-vuh-ree) The system of one person "owning" another.

surrendered (suh-REN-derd) Gave up.

Index

C

childhood, 4
compromise(s), 9
Confederate States
    of America, 14

D

debates, 12–13

I

Illinois, 7, 10
Illinois General
    Assembly, 10

K

Kentucky, 6, 22

L

Lee, Robert E., 19

N

nation, 5, 18, 21
nicknames, 4

P

president, 5, 13–14,
    21–22

S

settlers, 6
slavery, 5, 8–9, 12, 21
speaker, 5

U

United States, 8, 13,
    18, 21–22

W

war, 5, 15–16, 19,
    21
work, 4

Web Sites

Due to the changing nature of Internet links, PowerKids Press has developed an online list of Web sites related to the subject of this book. This site is updated regularly. Please use this link to access the list:
www.powerkidslinks.com/life/lincoln/